W9-CUO-043

With love and
warm memories
Love, Mom & Dad

Christmas 1998

Published by Petunia Press, Inc.,
407 Bridge Street, Charlevoix, Michigan 49720
(616) 547-7323

Text © 1998 by Dianne Foster
Photography © 1998 by Ken Scott
Earl Young photo on page 99 courtesy the *Charlevoix Courier*

Individual prints of the photographs in this book are available for
purchase directly from the photographer. Write to: Ken Scott
Photography, PO Box 668, Suttons Bay, Michigan 49682, or call
(616) 271-6000. Email: kenscott@gtii.com

All rights reserved. No part of this book may be reproduced or
transmitted in any form or by any means, electronic or mechanical,
including photocopying, recording, or by any information storage and
retrieval system, without permission in writing from the publisher.

Library of Congress Catalog Card Number: 97 - 95105
ISBN 0-9662399-8-9
10 9 8 7 6 5 4 3 2 1
First Edition
First Printing, June, 1998
Printed in Singapore
Design by Nielsen Design Group, Traverse City, Michigan

Charlevoix

MICHIGAN

Best Wishes
Dianne Foster '98
Enjoy!
Ken Scott '98

Charlevoix

MICHIGAN

Photography by KEN SCOTT

Text by DIANNE FOSTER

Published by PETUNIA PRESS

'Thru exposure we develop…

With dedication and much thanks to two teachers
who have influenced my journey:

Mr. Dave Andon… "Nothing to it, but to do it"
and Mr. Louis Prieskorn…

In memory of: Terry Woods (7/7/52-1/8/96)…

And, with continued
appreciation of my family…

KEN SCOTT

For my parents,
Don and Barb Reynolds. The most treasured gifts
you've shared are your love, time, laughter, patience,
and wisdom. In those moments I have always found
the courage.

Also for, my son, Hal.
Nothing will ever match the love, pride, satisfaction,
and pure joy that comes with being your mom.

DIANNE FOSTER

Contents

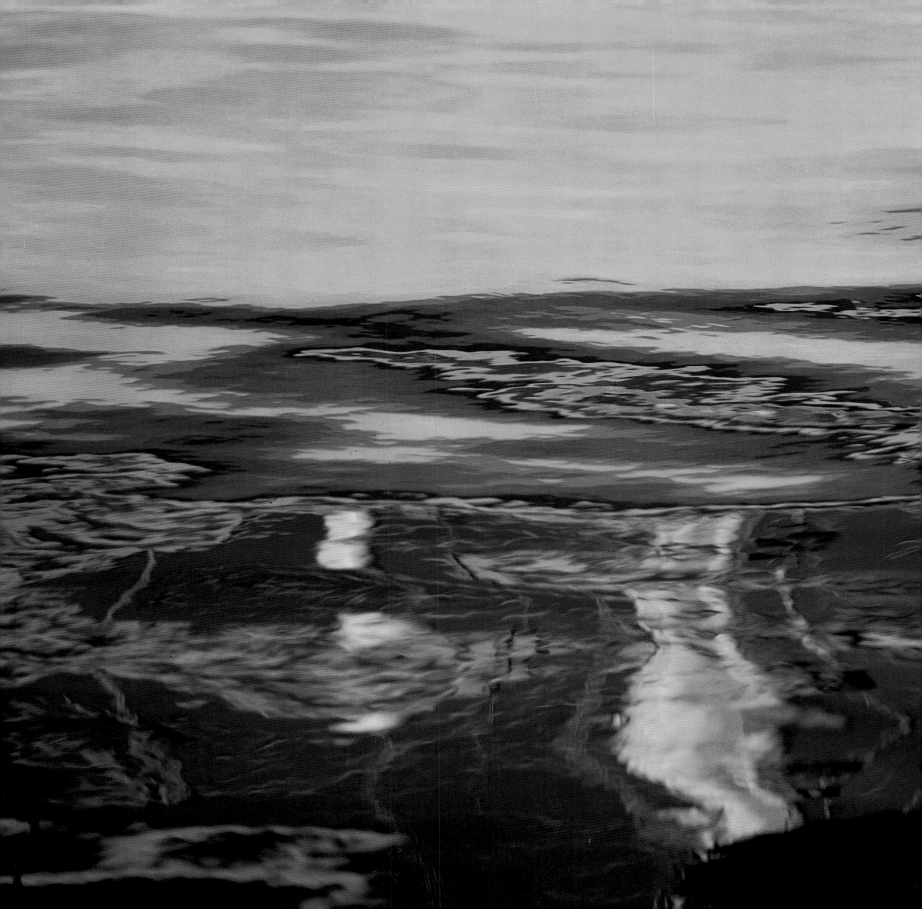

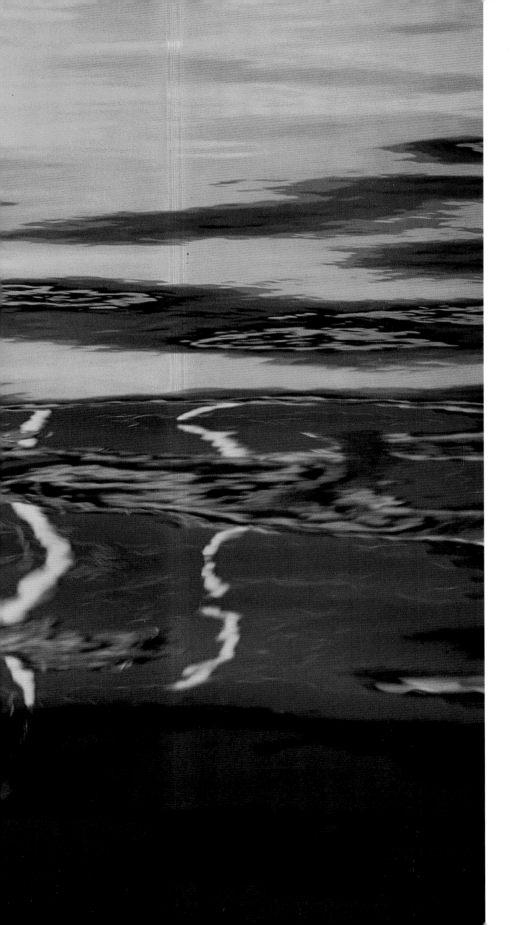

Charlevoix

AN INTRODUCTION

Strolling the waterfront in the archetypal harbor town of Charlevoix,
in the stillness of the morning, one is struck by its peaceful charm. For that moment
it is easy to imagine the whole world to be a place of breathtaking beauty.

Enveloped by three lakes – Lake Michigan, Round Lake, and
Lake Charlevoix – in the northwest corner of Michigan's Lower Peninsula,
Charlevoix County boasts the longest shoreline in Michigan.

Following this extensive shoreline in search of the elusive northwest passage, Father Pierre Francois-Xavier de Charlevoix, a French Jesuit missionary for whom the town is named, arrived here in 1721. Unlike Father Charlevoix, who continued his futile journey, many who discovered Charlevoix returned – or stayed.

Casual resorters, summer cottagers, and nearly 23,000 year-around residents are haunted by its beauty, intrigued by its history, and captivated by its recreational amenities. Charlevoix is a unique region of which people just cannot seem to get enough.

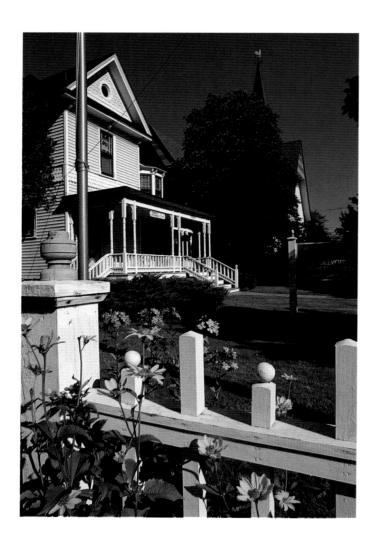

Sailors and fishermen have long watched the moods of the waters surrounding Charlevoix County. Each of the county's distinct communities – Beaver Island, Horton Bay, Norwood, East Jordan, Boyne City, Boyne Falls, Walloon Lake, and the county seat, Charlevoix – share a heritage of the lakes and forests.

*In the wake of explorers came fur traders, fishermen, settlers, farmers,
lumber barons, and manufacturers. Tourism and summer resorts followed in the late
nineteenth century and brought an economic balance to the region.*

It's hard to imagine the resort community of Charlevoix as once largely farmland.

However, long before upscale shops, fine restaurants, and glamorous yachts lined the valley, the

frontier business district was referred to by locals as the Mason-Dixon line. Most of the

north side was a farm owned by John S. Dixon and the south side was a farm belonging to Seth

Mason. The farms are long gone, but Dixon Avenue and Mason Street still mark the

north and south ends of the five-block downtown district.

While the waterfront remains the showpiece of the county, one need not wander far to discover that pastoral pleasures remain.

Country roads, wilderness trails, natural scenic rivers, secluded beaches, wildflower
meadows, farms, rustic campsites, and nature preserves still draw tens of thousands of visitors
seeking north woods solitude and outdoor recreation. Because of its many
shades of inspiring beauty, the region has long been a haven for writers and artists.

The Charlevoix region offers a complex climate of changes. The calendar becomes an arbitrary entity, for the seasons are measured by visual cues. Summertime begins when schools dismiss in June and tourists and summer residents flock to the area until Labor Day.

Fall arrives when the forested countryside bursts into spectacular color bringing tour buses from across the nation and visitors from around the world.

The undulating terrain becomes snow-covered in November and the region is in full swing with a multitude of wintertime activities by early December.

Spring is a season of renewal marked by significant events in each community.
It's spring in Charlevoix when the Dairy Queen opens; spring is heralded on Beaver Island
when the first ferry arrives; in Horton Bay it's spring when the General Store unlocks its
screen door; in the Boynes when the last square inch of snow melts on the infamous ski-run known
as "Hemlock" spring has arrived; and, in East Jordan it's spring when the steelhead trout
instinctively return to their home waters at the mouth of the Jordan River.

Charlevoix has captured hearts for generations. Its moods fluctuate,
its towns are diverse, its people are resilient, friendly, and fun-loving, but its natural
beauty and lack of big-city complexities are its most alluring qualities.

Visitors arrive here to lose themselves or, perhaps, to find themselves. Some arrive

merely to enjoy a change of scenery where the clouds seem closer, the stars brighter, and the pace

slower. Whether it's a weekend rendezvous, a summer retreat, or a lifetime of being held

in its charms, it's a beautiful corner of the world that is always difficult to leave.

Charlevoix

D I S C O V E R I E S

Charlevoix Light

THE FIRST CHARLEVOIX LIGHTHOUSE was built in 1885 on the north pier of the Pine River Channel. Since 1911, a lighthouse has been located on the south pier.

Today's Charlevoix lighthouse is one of the newer lights on the Great Lakes. Constructed in 1948, this active light has a rather unusual open steel base framework which protects the structure from wave action. The lighthouse was red until the 1960s when it was painted white. The steel and concrete pier replaced an old wooden catwalk in 1989.

The 100-candle power light constantly shines its red beacon. With a visibility of ten miles, the light is a land guide for vessels navigating Lake Michigan, and serves as a welcoming, warm glow of a porch light for sailors returning home.

The Petunia Story

CHARLEVOIX'S 50,000 PETUNIAS are at their luxuriant best on a mid-summer day, greeting all who enter the city limits. This colorful array of flowers lining four miles of U.S. 31, Charlevoix's bustling main thoroughfare, has earned national acclaim as an example of community pride.

"Operation Petunia" began in 1982 when Charlevoix native Dale Boss shared his vision for a more beautiful Charlevoix. In the dead of winter, volunteers chauffeured high school students door-to-door selling custom license plates designed by Marilyn Boss. In less than three hours the needed funds were raised to enact a masterful plan – a plan that would become Charlevoix tradition.

When the snow melted and the ground thawed, plenty of work was needed to prepare the roadside for planting. Many years of winter road maintenance with sand and salt had raised the soil up to eight inches higher than the curb. However, local contractors were undaunted by the arduous task of voluntarily removing 500 cubic yards of dirt to create flower beds for the first annual petunia planting.

In May, 1982, with trowels in hand, 450 volunteers arrived on the scene to plant 600 flats of petunias. Dale and Marilyn Boss assumed the daily watering chore by transforming their flat-bed truck into a makeshift watering 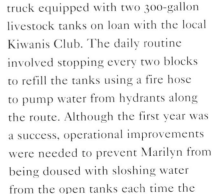 truck equipped with two 300-gallon livestock tanks on loan with the local Kiwanis Club. The daily routine involved stopping every two blocks to refill the tanks using a fire hose to pump water from hydrants along the route. Although the first year was a success, operational improvements were needed to prevent Marilyn from being doused with sloshing water from the open tanks each time the truck abruptly stopped or started.

The next year, the Charlevoix County State Bank donated a 1963, 2,000-gallon gasoline truck which was converted to a water truck. Marilyn stayed dry operating the water flow controls from the open passenger side of the truck while Dale maneuvered the truck up and down the petunia path.

The Keep Charlevoix Beautiful organization took
a sizable step toward enhancing "Operation Petunia" in 1986
with an auction and raffle which raised $22,000 to purchase a
custom-ordered, 1987 Ford truck. David Arnold, a local
welding craftsman, manufactured a 2,500-gallon tank for the

*"Operation Petunia" started
with one man's vision and has become
an annual celebration.*

truck. The truck,
decoratively hand-
lettered and displaying
petunias painted by
Marilyn Boss, is a
showpiece in parades
throughout the state to promote "Charlevoix the Beautiful."

In 1990, additional improvements to the tune of $10,500
lengthened the truck and added a new passenger cabin
to carry the Charlevoix Venetian Queen and her court in
parades. The truck, with all its bells and whistles, plays rag-
time piano music from four custom speakers built into the
side of the tank. Logging 4,500 miles a year, the petunia

water truck delivers a generous 12,000 to 15,000 gallons of
water to the petunias every morning from late May through
mid-September.

Today, the flower beds are prepared for planting each
spring by City of Charlevoix employees. The petunias,
grown locally, are the flowers of choice for their full season
blooming, and are maintained through the efforts of devoted
workers hired by Keep Charlevoix Beautiful.

Petunia planting springs into action at 5 o'clock in the
afternoon on the Thursday before Memorial Day, weather
permitting. The highway narrows to a single lane of traffic as
hundreds of volunteers of all ages work diligently to plant
1,000 flats of petunias in approximately two hours. When the
planting is done, the community celebrates their accomplish-
ment with a picnic in East Park. "Operation Petunia" started
with one man's vision and has become an annual celebration
of a certain magic that connects the people of Charlevoix.

Greensky Hill Church

PETER GREENSKY, A CHIPPEWA INDIAN, grew up at the Bay Mills Reservation near Sault Ste. Marie and attended a Methodist Indian school where he learned to speak, read, and write English.

During the 1830s, Reverend Peter Daugherty and Reverend John Fleming established the first Protestant Indian mission in the Grand Traverse Bay region. Greensky was invited to the Old Mission Peninsula, by Daugherty, to teach English to the Ottawa Indians. Greensky was an admired teacher and developed a following of what would become the Greensky Indians.

Greensky's reputation flourished and many more Indians found their way to Greensky Hill.

The Greensky Indians becoming disenchanted with the Traverse mission headed northward to Charlevoix. Leaving their canoes on the beach of Lake Charlevoix's Oyster Bay, the Indians trekked about two miles inland to discover a hill overlooking a small lake. The hill was aptly named Greensky Hill and the lake was named Susan, in honor of Greensky's wife.

The original mission church, built on this site, was an Elm bark wigwam, but as Greensky's reputation flourished and many more Indians found their way to Greensky Hill, a larger church was needed. Ten years in the building, the church was completed in the 1850s. The Greensky Indians constructed it of hand-hewn timber which they brought by canoe from Traverse City and then carried two miles over land to the site.

The Greensky Hill United Methodist Church, a Registered Michigan Historic Site, is located in an idyllic setting five miles from Charlevoix on Old Highway 31. Just beyond the winding dirt road to the church, on private land, eight crooked trees stand in a circle. Referred to as Council Trees, many legends are told about the meaning of this circle of trees. It is said, when the trees were twelve feet tall, the Indians used strips of basswood bark to bend the trees, making them grow crooked and thus undesirable to the lumbering white man.

Between the church and Susan Lake lies a burial ground where several hundred Native Americans are buried. Many of the wooden grave markers have disintegrated and the names etched in cement on cobblestone markers have washed away with more than a century of rain and snowfall. Although in 1864, Greensky was buried in this cemetery, his burial site is unknown.

The outdoor amphitheater is used for summer worship and camp Meetings. Methodist services for the Indian congregation at Greensky Church are held regularly throughout the year and visitors are welcome.

Charlevoix Train Depot

PRIOR TO 1892, GETTING TO CHARLEVOIX was a difficult journey for northbound travelers. A typical itinerary included the Grand Rapids and Indiana Railroad to Boyne Falls where passengers would transfer to a stagecoach departing for Boyne City, and then board a steamboat – the *Gazelle, Nellie Booth*, or *Clara Belle* – bound for Charlevoix. Others may have traveled north via rail to Traverse City, East Jordan, or Petoskey and then shuttled across water by steamers to Charlevoix. A few traveled on the steamship *Champlain* all the way from Chicago. In any case, there was nothing easy about getting to Charlevoix and when the first Iron Horse rolled into Charlevoix on June 26, 1892, it was a day of rejoicing for resorters who had long endured the hardships of traveling north.

A railroad swing bridge crossed the channel at the east end of Round Lake. A second depot, the Belvedere Station, was built just south of the trestle so that resorters could disembark the train within site of their cottages. The Belvedere Station mysteriously burned to the ground in 1931 and was not rebuilt.

During the summer there were three passenger trains to and from Grand Rapids, with connections to Chicago and Detroit. In 1900, the Chicago and Western Michigan Railroad merged with two other railroads to form the Pere Marquette Railroad. The Resort Special, a night train, was added to the schedule taking passengers comfortably by coach or sleeping car from Charlevoix to Detroit or on to Chicago. In 1947, the Pere Marquette Railroad merged with the Chesapeake and Ohio Railroad. The Resort Special was curtailed to only once a week until it was eliminated in 1958.

The last passenger train came to Charlevoix in 1962, and the last C & O freight train through Charlevoix was in 1982 before the C & O abandoned all lines north of Manistee. In 1984 the old railroad swing bridge was removed.

The depot's location on the shores of Lake Charlevoix made it a desirable home for the Charlevoix Yacht Club for several years. When a new Yacht Club was built, rather than allow the vacant depot to slide into ruinous decline, the Charlevoix Historical Society acquired the depot and completed its restoration to original beauty in 1997. Although a train whistle is no longer heard in Charlevoix, the depot still breathes its history, heritage and romance as a Museum open to the public.

Belvedere Club

THE BELVEDERE CLUB IS A PLACE where past meets present. It is a community of tree-lined streets, immense sweeps of lawn, unparalleled views of the lake, and enchanting century-old cottages curtained in sun-faded chintz and fanciful trim with heartbeats all their own. It's a private summer resort that resonates with family memories and Club traditions that are handed down, like heirlooms, from one generation to the next. For many, it's a quieter home-away-from-home that is tucked in some chamber of the heart for the nine or ten months of the year that are spent in cities far from Charlevoix.

The Belvedere Club was the first Charlevoix summer resort association, established by a small group of Baptist ministers and teachers from Kalamazoo, Michigan. For many Belvedere residents, their first introduction to the Belvedere was a stay at the grand old rambling Belvedere Hotel, or as a cottage renter, or an invited cottage guest at one of the eighty-seven cottages. Children, lots of children, and the beauty of Charlevoix is what enticed many families to the Belvedere. It has been the Shangri-La of youth for many generations of children who were Belvedere "gangsters." Here children, many of whom become lifelong friends, learn to play tennis, fish, water-ski, golf, or skipper a boat. They

learn to be good swimmers, campers, hikers, or dancers. Whether it's one summer or a life of summers, the experience becomes a treasured memory for the children of the Belvedere Club.

If you ask someone what has changed in fifty summers at the Belvedere they are likely to reply that "the trees are taller."

With the removal of the old Hotel in 1960, the Casino became the social center of the Belvedere Club. Whether a children's dance or masquerade, monthly Bingo, Wednesday Bridge, an annual cabaret, a July 4th celebration, Friday night dinner, or golf and tennis awards presentations, the Casino is a lively place for Belvedere Club members during the summer. While there is a whole lot of strolling, relaxing on the beach, and twilight porch-sitting

going on in the Belvedere, there has always been easy camaraderie and good-natured fun and festivities among friends and family to fill a long summer day.

The Belvedere Golf Club, located on Marion Center Road, is a beautiful eighteen-hole course designed by William Watson and landscaped by Vern Miller. The Golf Club was privileged to host the prestigious Michigan Amateur Golf Tournament for twenty-seven years until 1989 when the tournament began rotating to sites throughout the state.

In a world that is constantly changing, if you ask someone what has changed in fifty summers at the Belvedere they are likely to reply that "the trees are taller." For most of us, it is deeply satisfying to feel the links that bind us to our past, and we find comfort in knowing that life keeps repeating itself. The Belvedere Club has filled many hearts with that kind of satisfaction.

Chicago Club

In the fall of 1880, members of the First Congregational Church, Chicago, established Charlevoix's second summer resort association. The Chicago Club resides on forty acres of what was once part of the Dixon Terrace Farm. Sitting high on the sloping terrain, fronting Lake Charlevoix and Round Lake, gentle summer breezes and captivating views of the lakes provide a gorgeous setting for this peaceful resort.

The majestic Club House and five or six stylish cottages were built in 1881. The Club House originally provided twenty-seven comfortable sleeping rooms, a ladies' sitting room, a gentlemen's club room, and a spacious dining room serving three meals a day. Today, tried-and-true customs still prevail such as the traditional Sunday evening hymn sing and buffet.

Gentle summer breezes and captivating views of the lakes provide a gorgeous setting for this peaceful resort.

When the Club House has been vacated in favor of the beach or tennis courts on a midsummer's day, its rooms remain comfortably occupied with the mingled images of past and present. Shafts of sunlight flow through its windows casting a warm, friendly glow on summer reading savored, devoured, and discussed by residents and guests just as they have done for many decades. Shadows dance with timeworn photographs that preserve the cheerfulness of early cottage owners. Bulletins announce Club news and upcoming events. One can easily discover the pleasure of good company in a place enveloped with history and promise.

In 1896, Chicago Club members John P. Watson and Edward C. Waller founded the Chicago Club Golf Course. Designed by renowned golf course architect William Watson, the original nine-hole course was expanded in 1903 to eighteen holes. When golf play declined, the Chicago Club generously sold their golf course in 1937 to the City of Charlevoix for one dollar. The public has long enjoyed play on this beautiful nine-hole Municipal Golf Course. The city converted the second nine holes of the golf course to an industrial park.

Chicago Club residents arrive today from all parts of the country and continue to appreciate quiet, healthy summers of rest, relaxation, and recreation. Boating, tennis, golf, bicycling, swimming, or simply walking the grounds with a beloved family pet are popular pastimes. Children burn endless energy in supervised play, organized learning activities, and instructional sports tailored for the "crews" of the Chicago Club.

The Chicago Club is surrounded by the sparkling green and blue hues of the lakes, twenty-eight cottages, a glistening boathouse, and a Club House, all subtly graced in romantic charm and memories of days past. In its midst, one is touched in the most sentient reaches of the mind knowing that this idyllic place has been treasured, shared, and meticulously cared for by generations of families and friends who have made Charlevoix their summer home.

Sequanota Club

SEEN ONLY FROM LAKE CHARLEVOIX, between Two Mile Point and Ironton, eyes are drawn to twenty-two cottages decorously lining the precipitous landscape. Serene and understated, Sequanota Club bespeaks a casual tone and comfortable character time can only improve.

Sequanota is a Native American word meaning "many springs." However, cottage lore is that Sequanota is a play on the Latin words for "sequence of music notes," composed by one of the Club's founders, John Winter Thompson, who was a professor of music at the Knox Conservatory in Galesburg, Illinois.

Here the hum of traffic has vanished and city lights are replaced with starlit skies.

Founded in 1902 by professors and preachers from Galesburg and Macomb, Illinois, Sequanota Club was started with thirteen cottages. In 1927, when the number of cottages reached twenty-two, it was decided that the Club would expand no further keeping a sense of intimacy and providing a lake view from each cottage. A Club House was built in 1903 and is still enjoyed by members for meals, games, and festivities.

Like other resort associations, residents come to Sequanota to disengage from the torrid summer heat and abrading affects of bigger cities and to enjoy secluded time with family and friends. Here the hum of traffic has vanished and city lights are replaced with starlit skies. One can easily succumb to porch-sitting apathy in a wicker chair surrounded only by the sounds of twittering birds in the trees, the laughter of children on the beach, the peaceful lull of waves washing ashore, and the sporadic drone of an outboard motor on the lake.

As the sun rises over Lake Charlevoix, the tranquil cottages are bejeweled in its glow and the stillness of the morning is impressive. In the solitude of this snug haven, during a moment so sublime as sunrise, it is easy to understand why one returns, summer after summer, to the warmth of Sequanota.

Loeb Farm

ALBERT LOEB WAS A MAN OF GREAT COMPASSION and progressive ideas. As a practicing attorney in Chicago, one of his early clients was Julius Rosenwald, owner of Sears Roebuck Company. Rosenwald was impressed with Loeb's intellect, kindness, and forward thinking and persuaded him to become a Vice President for Sears Roebuck Company. Among Loeb's greatest contributions to the company were the establishment of a profit-sharing program for company employees and the development of an experimental farm using Sears Roebuck's newest equipment.

Two miles east of Charlevoix, on Highway 66, Loeb and his wife, Anna, built their beautiful farm fronting the south shore of Lake Charlevoix on 1,300 acres.

Loeb's longing for a model farm, where his family could enjoy cooler summers and where blooded livestock would be bred and raised, became a reality in 1917 despite World War I and its ensuing hardships. Two miles east of Charlevoix, on Highway 66, Loeb and his wife, Anna, built their beautiful farm fronting the south shore of Lake Charlevoix on 1,300 acres.

The barns, two houses, and gate houses of "Stone Farm," as it was affectionately known, are detailed with steep roofs, dormers, cupolas, towers, flying buttresses, arches, cobblestone courtyards, and a fountain springing from an artesian well. The farm's architecture, designed by well-known Chicago architect Arthur Heun, was created with area fieldstone and hardwoods. It embodies the medieval best of the chateaux found throughout the Normandy region of France.

During its heyday, the grounds hummed with activity as ninety employees nurtured livestock, Belgian horses, flower and vegetable gardens, and apple orchards. A baseball diamond was the site of lively Saturday afternoon games. Enthralled families strolled the grounds, savoring an aura of old-world romance blended with heartland promise. Golden Leader Cheddar Cheese, ice cream, fruits and vegetables, and fresh-cut flowers were favorite purchases at the farm. Visiting artists often set up easels and whiled away their time painting animals, colorful landscapes, and the distinctive buildings. The farm's cattle and Belgian horses won national awards and innovative farming methods captured widespread attention.

Albert Loeb and his son, Ernest, were greatly admired by the farm's employees for their caring and personable

leadership. Ernest lived year-around on the farm and, prior to his marriage, shared living quarters and meals with the workers. They worked, sweated, laughed, learned, and prospered together in a family-oriented, innovative environment that was especially inspiring for its time.

When Albert Loeb died in 1924, Ernest continued the farming enterprise. Then the Great Depression peaked and farming operations fell into decline. Although the local community was very loyal to the farm, a market beyond the local economy was needed to generate the revenues required to sustain the farm. Additionally, without refrigerated railroad cars, dairy products could not be easily transported to bigger cities. The livestock was sold in 1927, sadly ending a golden era for the community and Loeb Farm. The Loeb family retained the farm, although it was relatively idle, for three decades.

In 1961, the Loeb family sold a 100-acre parcel of the

Albert Loeb and his son, Ernest, were greatly admired by the farm's employees for their caring and personable leadership.

farm, including the barns, to John van Haver, an artist skilled in bronze casting with a passion for architecture, landscaping, and Medieval artifacts. Van Haver began, but did not complete, restoration of the barns to their original splendor and "Castle van Haver" became a tourist attraction.

In 1968, the farm changed hands again when it was sold to Arthur Reibel, a Detroit lawyer. It became "Castle Farms" known for its controversial big-name, big-sound rock and roll concerts of the 1970s and 1980s, staged in its outdoor amphitheater. In the 1990s it transformed, under the same ownership, to a series of retail shops featuring regional wines, gourmet foods, and the varied creations of Michigan artists. Activities, drawing thousands of curious visitors, have included Renaissance festivals, art fairs, and antique shows as Castle Farms has attempted to create a new image and find a lasting niche in today's environment.

The magical buildings of Loeb Farm remain a treasured Charlevoix landmark. Regardless of what the future may hold, the happy memories of Loeb Farm, and what it represented economically and pleasurably during an otherwise depressed era, have left an indelible mark on the history of Charlevoix.

Ironton Ferry

SINCE 1883, A CABLE-GUIDED FERRY has provided transportation across the 700-foot channel that separates the west shore of Lake Charlevoix's South Arm at Ironton from the east shore at Hemingway Point on the peninsula. The three minute ferry trip saves a sixteen mile drive around the South Arm and is a common shortcut from Charlevoix to Hemingway Point.

Shuttling a maximum load of four vehicles, the ferry makes over 200 trips on a busy summer day.

Shuttling a maximum load of four vehicles, the ferry makes over 200 trips on a busy summer day.

Since 1981, the Ironton Ferry has been operated by the Charlevoix County Transportation Authority and the Charlevoix County Road Commission which charges nominal toll fees to cover operating expenses. During winter, some residents who make regular commutes keep one car on either side of the narrow channel and walk across the ice to avoid the long drive around the lake. Designated a "Michigan Historical Site," the Ironton Ferry has been granted a permanent presence and will continue to traverse "the narrows" from mid-April to December each year.

Sam Alexander is credited with making the Ironton Ferry famous. Mr. Alexander was hired by the County of Charlevoix to operate the ferry from 1911 until his retirement in 1942. During that time, Robert E. Ripley's "Believe It Or Not" column ran in newspapers coast to coast stating that, in performing his job, Mr. Alexander had traveled more than 15,000 miles and was never farther than 1,000 feet from his home.

John Cross Fisheries

TUCKED AMONG SHOWY YACHTS and million dollar homes on Round Lake, John Cross Fisheries brings a character to the harbor that cannot be matched nor mimicked. Its character lies in history, and that history runs deep.

The landmark fishery, at 209 Belvedere Avenue, has been a Charlevoix institution for locals, summer residents, and tourists since 1941. The place bustles with people in rubber boots and gloves cleaning, smoking, and packaging fresh fish. The phone never stops ringing. Orders are filled daily for eager customers lined up at the market's little counter, and deliveries are made to over thirty restaurants and markets in northwest Michigan. Time and time again, the nostalgic remark is sounded, "Don't change a thing – this is exactly what a fish market should look like!"

At one time, between 1920 and 1940, there were twenty established commercial fisheries in Charlevoix. Today there is only one.

Born in 1897, John Cross was the oldest of nine brothers in a family of sixteen children. Cross began fishing as a young boy off the shores of Beaver Island. Originally from Benton Harbor, Michigan, the Cross family moved to Beaver Island at about the turn of the century, and settled in Charlevoix in 1910. The nine brothers each had a boat and sold their netted fish to wholesalers. At one time, between 1920 and 1940, there were twenty established commercial fisheries in Charlevoix. Today there is only one.

When Cross founded his fishery in 1941, his wife, Hulda, opened The Nautical restaurant in a house on the same lot. Although the restaurant closed in 1972, many folks can still taste the whitefish, trout, hush puppies, carrot salad, coleslaw, homemade breads, bisque, and lemon pie – all you could eat for $2.25. Today, whitefish remains a popular selection on the menu at area restaurants, and June Cross's smoked whitefish pate is a perennial favorite at the market.

Before federal regulations changed, allowing only Native Americans to set fishing nets in American waters of the Great Lakes, Cross Fisheries operated with two boats. The wooden *Jackie C* and the steel-hulled, enclosed fishing tug *Jackie II* were workhorses on Lake Michigan. Hardy crews weathered rough waters, lifting and pulling nets. It was

rigorous, but satisfying work even when the lake was calm.

John Cross fished for seventy years. He worked and fought hard to survive the ups and downs of an industry wrought with nature-induced hardships and changing laws. In 1986, at age eighty-nine, Mr. Cross was laid to rest with a picture of his boat inscribed on his headstone, and his family business immortalized by the faithful support of his community and the ambition of his loving family.

John Cross fished for seventy years. He worked and fought hard to survive the ups and downs of an industry wrought with nature-induced hardships.

Today, the fishery is owned and operated by John Jr. ("Jack") and his wife, June, along with their children, son, John III ("Jackie") and, daughter and son-in-law, Kellie and Jack Sutherland. During the peak season, three or four employees join the family to meet the demands of the business.

When the old fishing boats, the *Sunny Don* and *Jerry W,* quietly make their way through the harbor, carrying local Native Americans delivering their day's catch to Cross Fisheries, the air becomes clamorous with the sound of swooping gulls. It's a scene one never tires of – a scene that reassures there will be whitefish served tonight. Fresh fish is also picked up, by truck, at Peshawbestown, on the Leelanau Peninsula, and in Mackinac City. When the northern Michigan season slows, the fishery sends fresh fish to markets in Detroit and Chicago.

Whitefish is to Charlevoix what lobster is to Maine and for over half a century John Cross Fisheries has been the first stop for many folks arriving in town, and remains a last stop for local folks heading home for the day.

Legendary Stone Houses

THE ILLUSTRIOUS ONE-OF-A-KIND STONE HOUSES in Charlevoix have a certain charm that evokes a response from every passerby. Cars slow to a snail's pace. Walkers halt and hover to get a closer look. Bikes pull over. Tour buses empty. Cameras click. It is a sightseer's extravaganza – one that elicits curiosity, delight, admiration, and pure fascination. It is, perhaps, the perpetuation of emotions felt by Earl Young for over five decades as he zealously created an architectural legacy in the town he loved.

Born in 1889, in Mancelona, Michigan, Earl A. Young moved to Charlevoix when he was about ten years old. An only child, he passed time with playmates sauntering shorelines to collect interesting rocks. This childhood pastime grew into a passion that led to a lifelong companionship with stones. After graduating from Charlevoix High School, Young briefly attended the University of Michigan with fleeting thoughts of pursuing a law degree. Instead, he returned to Charlevoix to operate an insurance agency with his mother. In 1915,

Young married his high school sweetheart, Irene Harsha, an accomplished pen and watercolor artist.

Young built a house for his growing family in 1921 – a stone house – at 304 Park Avenue. That house was the dawning of a dream that would change the face of Charlevoix.

Until his death in 1975, Young built or remodeled thirty picturesque stone houses and commercial structures without a blueprint. Young held a Michigan Real Estate Broker's license for sixty years. Not an architect or builder by education or license, Young subscribed to a handful of building and architectural magazines but was, otherwise, self-taught. He was an imaginative dreamer, designer, and demonstrative construction adviser. Stone became his art, the earth was his canvas, and a lack of formal training never hampered his ambition, skill, or creativity.

Country fields, dusty quarries, and long stretches of beach enticed Young for more than half a century of wandering as he kept a watchful eye for quarry limestone, granite

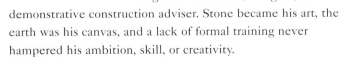

field stone and Onaway quarry stone. Young used red stone brought by barge from the Soo Locks area in Michigan's Upper Peninsula for the construction of two houses. Large boulders were a particular attraction for Young. He said on more than one occasion, "I have a very strong feeling for stone. Stones have their own personalities. People say I'm crazy when I say so, but really they do." Indeed, Young did have a special relationship with stones. If he did not have an immediate site for a treasured find he would have it hauled away, buried, dropped in the lake or hidden in the woods for future use. The history of large, old, glacial stones held a special appeal for Young. Sometimes he would chip off a sample and send it away to be identified and analyzed by geologists.

In 1924, Young purchased thirty-seven acres of land along the Lake Michigan shoreline, just beyond where the Charlevoix Area Hospital stands today. The property became Boulder Park with meandering little streets and eighty-five building sites. Prior to the Depression, Young erected an arca-

dia of twelve quaint stone houses sequestered among groves of towering birches and giant oaks. Stones and boulders garnish the lawns like hedges, shrubs, and fences of more conventional landscapes.

Young believed in designing a house to complement the natural setting. Trees weren't torn down – he worked around them. It was an art and every part of it had to be in harmony. Friends and family describe how he would carefully study the lot and then he would think and think about it. Sometimes he sketched an idea and other times he simply began building with a detailed plan in mind. If it wasn't just so, it came down and was rebuilt until it was right.

It was right when the structure matched Young's vision. Building it right was a joy for Young and a labor of love and satisfaction for the workers involved. While Young didn't actually build the houses, he was on-site directing a hand-selected crew of carpenters and stone masons – telling them precisely where each stone must be placed. Boulders were

selected for size, color, and shape. They had to be meticulously set and sometimes held in place by cranes for two or three days while the mortar hardened. Young once stated, "Detail, that's my success." His favorite subjects for scrupulous attention to detail were windows, doorways, chimneys and fireplaces. Penned in a 1973 interview with the *Detroit Free Press*, Young chided, "It drives them crazy. But I know what I want." In the same interview, he boasted that, at age 84, he had outlived six masons.

One of the most admired homes in Boulder Park is Boulder Manor. Constructed in the 1930s, the home was built with large glacial boulders, Onaway stone, and local limestone. It is one of the few Young homes built with thick interior stone walls. A children's playhouse, in the backyard, replicates the design of the house, including a working fireplace. Many of the other materials used in the construction of Young's homes were salvaged from demolition projects at the mansions of Chicago lumber barons. Like his precious stones,

Young would store the materials until he had just the right use for them.

Young's second development of homes are the eleven houses, built or remodeled in the 1940s and 1950s on the triangular block of Park, Clinton, and Grant streets. While some of the original designs have been altered, or original roofs replaced, every home retains distinguishable Young characteristics. During this era, Young's style had progressed away from angular roof lines. Roof shingles, several layers deep in some places, resulted in the undulated roof design. Young achieved the narrow stone effect in the house he built for himself at 306 Park Avenue, by laying Onaway stone on its side.

Jeannine Wallace purchased the "mushroom house" at 301 Grant Street, in 1964. Her appreciation for Young's art and originality runs deep as she describes feeling "like the keeper of someplace very special." In the early 1980s, Wallace replaced the roof with the same diligent care that Young would have shown. She located the original roof supplier in

Michigan's Upper Peninsula to provide the cedar shake shingles. With several photographs of the original roof, a few men, and many weeks of work the roof was replaced and Wallace is certain that "Earl would have been pleased."

In 1954, Young fulfilled a ten year dream to purchase the ninety year old, three-story, metal covered Argo grist mill on the Pine River Channel. The flour mill was stripped, leaving only the original foundation and timbers on the main floor intact.

When asked what was his favorite building of all, Young simply smiled and said, "My next one."

The site became the Weathervane Inn. Young loved the Weathervane Inn so much that he kept an office on the lower level until his death. The Fountain City House, a hotel just north of where the grist mill stood, was acquired by Young and demolished to become the site of the Weathervane Terrace.

The Weathervane Inn presented Young the long-awaited opportunity to use his favorite stone. Found in 1928 during a street excavation project, Young had buried the mammoth rock, weighing 18,260 pounds, for twenty-six years and kept the measurements in his head. Young instructed workers to leave enough space in the rafters of the restaurant to lower the boulder into place. When the stone wouldn't pass through the opening, Young chuckled and offered only one explanation to the frustrated workmen, "It grew eleven inches during all those years in the woods." The giant stone, shaped like a map of lower Michigan, is the keystone in the restaurant's main dining room fireplace.

Another piece in the fireplace is a meteorite of iron. The Inn's outside signpost is also decorated with a meteorite. The main floor bar is constructed from pieces of an old shipwreck, the tables are made from walnut stumps, and the lights outside of the Weathervane Inn came from Copenhagen, Denmark many, many decades ago. Young

admitted on several occasions, "I really put myself into the Weathervane." Although, during an interview less than two years prior to his death, when asked what was his favorite building of all, he simply smiled and said, "My next one."

Young was involved in two other commercial ventures, including the design of The Lodge hotel and the front of the Apple Tree gift shop on Bridge Street. He was also the catalyst behind the development of East Park on Round Lake. His last three homes were constructed in the late 1960s, edging the north shore of Round Lake, on Thistle Down. To the horror of many Charlevoix residents, one Young home on Thistle Down was purchased and demolished in the mid-1990s to use the property as a building site for a new home.

The Earl Young homes are such an attraction that the Charlevoix Chamber of Commerce provides a brochure, with a detailed map for a self-guided driving tour. Living in a tourist attraction is, at times, an awkward dance for the residents of these private homes. It's a dance of pride of ownership and preservation of privacy. With each season the steps hasten or slow as the music changes pace. One homeowner summarized, "The occasional intrusions never overshadow the pleasures. I've been here for nearly forty years and I wouldn't trade my home for the world. Most people are very considerate in their curiosity. I think Earl built these homes to be looked at, enjoyed, and lived in. I try to honor that."

Earl Young loved the city of Charlevoix. Although he had been asked many times to design and build houses throughout the country, only once he relented and built a home for a friend in Alma, Michigan. Young promoted Charlevoix throughout the world on pleasure and business trips, but he chose to make his statement, to create his art, where his heart was. For Charlevoix, that has made all the difference.

Young promoted Charlevoix throughout the world on pleasure and business trips, but he chose to make his statement, to create his art, where his heart was.

Big Rock Point
1962-1997

....

As part of the Atomic Energy Commission's
research program, Big Rock Point developed more efficient
nuclear fuels for the commercial nuclear power industry.
The plant's reactor was also employed to produce radioactive
cobalt for medicine and industry.

Designated a Nuclear Historic Landmark, Big
Rock Point was the world's first high power density boiling
water reactor and became the longest running nuclear
plant in the United States in 1993. To their credit, Big Rock
Point employees achieved twenty years without a lost
time accident.

Big Rock Point was shut down on August 29, 1997
at 10:22 a.m.

United States Coast Guard

THE CHARLEVOIX HARBOR, with its channel and three lakes, is a boat watcher's paradise. Every day of the summer a new scene emerges as vessels of all shapes, sizes, and vintage ply the waters. As boating season follows boating season many familiar launches return, but one vessel that is ever present is the U.S. Coast Guard Cutter *Acacia*, the "Ace of the Lakes."

Station Charlevoix is a small boat station with a big mission.

A U.S. Life Saving Station, established in Charlevoix in 1899, was commissioned on July 5, 1900. In 1915, the government renamed the function the United States Coast Guard. In the early 1960s the U.S. Coast Guard Station Charlevoix was relocated from the west end of the Pine River Channel to the east end, where it stands today, at the confluence of Round Lake and Lake Charlevoix. The old Life Saving Station was demolished in 1965.

Station Charlevoix is a small boat station with a big mission. The sixteen-member crew is responsible for year-round search and rescue missions, law enforcement, public safety, education, and environmental protection. Station Charlevoix has an area of operation extending over 2,500 square miles of inland waterways, small lakes, and 45 miles out from the pierheads into the unpredictable waters of Lake Michigan, making the station one of the busiest under Group Sault Ste. Marie.

Training is a year-round activity involving operational drills, departmental reviews, helicopter operations, and ice-rescue simulations. The station is home to a 41-foot utility boat, a 21-foot rigid hull inflatable boat, and a 14-foot ice skiff.

The Coast Guard Auxiliary, numbering slightly more than the station crew, is a critical support to the active duty crew of the U.S. Coast Guard. Established in Charlevoix in 1946, the men and women volunteers actively participate in training and stand ready to assist in search and rescue missions. Qualified Auxiliary also assist in radio watchstand. They teach Boating and Water Safety Programs, provide vessel examination, and patrol the lakes and shorelines. On a typical summer weekend, Auxiliary boats are located in Lake Charlevoix, East and West Grand Traverse Bays, and Little Traverse Bay on alert and ready to offer assistance to vessels in distress.

Charlevoix has been home port to a Coast Guard Cutter

since 1977 with the arrival of the U.S. Coast Guard Cutter *Mesquite*, a World War II-vintage 180-foot buoy tender. The *Mesquite* left her home port on November 9, 1989 for what would be her last voyage. After the cold, dirty, brutal task of removing twenty-six buoys for the winter months, Lake Superior's treacherous Keweenaw Point claimed the *Mesquite* at 2:10 a.m. on December 4, 1989. There were no fatalities among the fifty-three crew members when the vessel grounded on rocks that gashed its hull. Ten days later, when salvage experts and divers reported that all hope of refloating and repairing the *Mesquite* was gone, she was decommissioned where she lay and later cut up and sunk as part of a diving attraction.

When the *Mesquite* was lost, Charlevoix campaigned diligently for a replacement vessel. In 1990, the *Acacia* (WLB 406) was moved from Grand Haven, Michigan to Charlevoix. With the exception of one year spent in Portland, Maine, the *Acacia* has been assigned to the Great Lakes since she was commissioned on September 1, 1944. Most buoy tenders are named for trees, shrubs, or other forms of vegetation. *Acacia* is named for a group of thorny trees in the legume family having clusters of small yellow or white flowers.

The Coast Guard Cutter *Acacia* is one of twenty-eight 180-foot seagoing buoy tenders built for the U.S. Coast Guard between 1942 and 1944. Built by the Zenith Dredge Company in Duluth, Minnesota during wartime, she originally carried a 3-inch gun plus 20-millimeter machine guns, as well as depth charge racks and projectors. The vessel is named after the Coast Guard Cutter *Acacia* which fell victim to the German U-boat *U-161* and sunk off the British West Indies in March, 1942. No lives were lost in the incident.

In 1975, the *Acacia* underwent major renovations, including the conversion of the ship's electronic boom system to hydraulics, installation of air conditioning, and the addition of a bow thruster. In 1987, the 42-year old main engines were replaced. The ship is now propelled by two 750-horsepower General Motors Electro-Motor Diesel Engines which drive two DC generators. Electricity is furnished to the 1200-horsepower electric motor which turns *Acacia*'s propeller for a maximum speed of 13 knots (15 mph). The ship's single stainless steel propeller is 9-feet, 6-inches in diameter with five blades.

The *Acacia*'s beam (width) is 37 feet and each of *Acacia*'s bow anchors weighs 2,225 pounds and have 720 feet of chain. The *Acacia* has a diesel fuel capacity of 28,000 gallons which

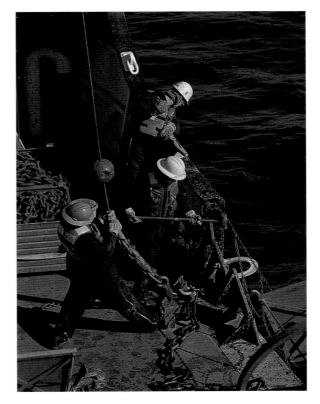

enables her to operate for up to one month without refueling. Her freshwater tanks supply over 30,000 gallons – enough water for ten days' normal operation.

The unique features which distinguish *Acacia* from other vessels are its icebreaker hull and hydraulically operated boom with a lifting capacity of 20 tons. Although the rounded hull with a blunt, stepped bow was designed for the ship to ride up on the ice and break through with her weight, the term Coast Guard "cutter" does not refer to ice breaking capabilities. "Cutter" originates from the sailing cutters that helped enforce the nation's early revenue laws. The term is applied today by the U.S. Coast Guard to all vessels more than 65 feet in length.

Acacia's primary duty is maintaining over 250 buoys, lighthouses, and other aids to navigation. Her area of operation extends from Chicago, Illinois on the south shore of Lake Michigan to Alpena, Michigan on northern Lake Huron. Among various other duties are search and rescue of lost or disabled vessels, ice breaking assistance, and aid to local emergency personnel in the times of disaster. She also works in cooperation with the National Oceanic and Atmospheric Administration efforts to acquire weather information. During peacetime the U.S. Coast Guard operates her under the direction of the U.S. Department of Transportation while in times of conflict her accountability shifts to the U.S. Department of Defense.

The U.S. Coast Guard Station and the *Acacia* bring approximately seventy enlisted men and women to Charlevoix. In addition to their primary mission of maintaining corridors of safe navigation, the Coast Guard is an integral and appreciated part of the local community. Crew members enthusiastically support community events, actively participate in school academic and sports programs, and create the popular Halloween "ghost ship" to the thrill of many children and adults. The crew at the Station and aboard the *Acacia* welcome opportunities to enlighten Charlevoix residents and visitors about the mission of the U.S. Coast Guard. Their presence in Charlevoix is a comfort and privilege that the people of Charlevoix County do not take lightly.

> Acacia's *primary duty is maintaining over 250 buoys, lighthouses, and other aids to navigation.*

Horton Bay & Hemingway

Nestled between Charlevoix and Boyne City is Horton Bay. As the road winds and folds into dells, past Susan Lake and along Lake Charlevoix, our eyes are drawn to magnificent old barns. We feel a gentleness in the open meadows, untouched and unadorned by the clutter of modern life. These same vistas could have been seen – were seen – a hundred years ago. It's as if nature is preparing us, mile by mile, for a tranquil step back in time as we reduce our speed and approach Horton Bay.

The pulse of activity in the "City on the Bay" has always been, and continues to be, the Horton Bay General Store.

History records that in 1843 Samuel Horton got lost on Lake Charlevoix while traveling by boat from Toledo, Ohio in search of Grand Rapids, Michigan. Seduced by the beauty of the region, he gave up his search and settled on the north shore of Lake Charlevoix. Officially founded in 1876, Horton's Bay grew as a lumbering and sawmill community. Despite the Post Office's elimination in 1894 of the possessive, many people mistakenly refer to the town as Horton's Bay, an immediate tip to residents and cottagers that a tourist has just arrived.

The pulse of activity in the "City on the Bay" has always been, and continues to be, the Horton Bay General Store. Listed on the National Register of Historic Places, the Store has continually operated since its establishment by William Ohle in 1876, and also served as the community Post Office for thirty years. Open from May through September or October, the General Store has achieved a measure of notoriety for its use as the setting of a national television commercial and documentary on "Hemingway in Northern Michigan." The Store has been featured in several magazines and there may be truth to the proclamation that the General Store is the most photographed store in North America. A favorite past time is reminiscing on the front porch or sitting at the lunch counter foraging through Ernest Hemingway memorabilia. A glance at the walls and ceiling of the Store is a lesson in local history, and each slam of the screen door evokes the mood of a time now past.

The General Store, and the entire town of Horton Bay, has a connection to Award-winning American author Ernest Hemingway. The connection started in 1900 when Hemingway's parents, Doctor Clarence Hemingway and

Grace Ernestine Hemingway of Oak Park, Illinois purchased land on Walloon Lake and built the family cottage. Walloon Lake, formerly called Bear Lake, is located four miles over the sandy hills from Horton Bay. The cottage may have been named "Windemere" for Grace Hemingway's fascination with Sir Walter Scott's novels. Overlooking Walloon Lake, shrouded from sight, "Windemere" remains in the Hemingway family as a private cottage.

From infancy to young adulthood Ernest Hemingway spent summers at Walloon Lake and his wanderings frequently carried him to Horton Bay. It is agreed by Hemingway scholars that Northern Michigan, and especially Horton Bay, served as a source of great inspiration and a backdrop for several Hemingway short stories. Hemingway's fondness for Northern Michigan as a vast, rugged, and wonderfully mysterious place for childhood experiences later merged into a literary kaleidoscope. Being in these surroundings, one becomes partner with the moods that swept young Hemingway from civilization to wilderness as he camped along the shore, fished the creeks and lakes, and wandered the woods and countryside.

Cottages that served as familiar havens to Hemingway

still stand on Lake Street. Neighboring cottages Pinehurst and Shangri-La, owned by Hemingway's friends Elizabeth and Jim Dilworth, were pivotal to the revitalization of Horton Bay when the lumbering industry waned. Elizabeth Dilworth served chicken dinners out of her Pinehurst home and then opened Shangri-La to house summer visitors. In 1921 these two charming cottages were the site of events surrounding Hemingway's first marriage to Hadley Richardson. Hemingway spent the night before his marriage at Pinehurst, and the couple celebrated their wedding breakfast at Shangri-La before retreating by row boat across Walloon Lake to the family cottage for their honeymoon. Although this familial summer retreat figures prominently in Hemingway's early life, it is believed that he spent little, if any, time in Northern Michigan after 1921.

When the buzzing of saws in Horton Bay was no longer heard, the pleasure of good food attracted visitors. The Red Fox Inn, just east of the General Store, was operated by Lizzie Fox as a boarding house for lumber men and transient guests. It was transformed into a popular dining establishment renowned for its chicken dinners and tomato pudding. Lizzie Fox's daughter, Marion Hartwell, continued to operate

the restaurant until the 1970s. People still speak fondly of memories at the Red Fox Inn.

The Alonzo Stroud house, just across the street from Pinehurst, was also a popular eatery. Kathryn Kennedy Dilworth created a waffle shop in the mid-1920s that drew crowds from near and far. Were it not for the tenacity of these three ladies, Horton Bay might have suffered the fate of other Northern Michigan lumbering towns. Instead, a resort community flourished creating jobs and boosting the town's economy.

Horton Bay has earned its reputation as "Home of the Best Little Fourth in the North."

This rich and fascinating history is perpetuated by the twenty-seven current townspeople and many cottagers whose vitality is showcased in the frolicsome events of Horton Bay. The premier annual event, organized by a group of local volunteers and local wannabes, is the Fourth of July parade which has become the biggest small town parade in the world. The parade forbids commercial entries and bans all politicians, except for the Sheriff who leads the parade. With silent marching bands, wacky floats, and brilliant comedy, the parade trots about 651 yards to the delight of thousands of spectators. This unique Independence Day celebration expresses a serious and deep respect for freedom played out with humor in high art form. Horton Bay has earned its reputation as "Home of the Best Little Fourth in the North."

In keeping with the spirit of a fiercely independent community, in 1991 Representative Robert W. Davis appealed to the United States House of Representatives to consider Horton Bay as the fifty-first State of the Union. He offered that their state motto be "Laughter is the Best Medicine." This act of Congress did not materialize, but that has never dampened the spirit of the fun-loving people of Horton Bay.

In late October, after the autumn colors have faded, the General Store creaks and groans as the wind goes around to the northwest. The snow falls and Horton Bay quietly slips into the short-day, long-night season with a kind of languid semi-hibernation. Early or late, usually creeping, spring always comes again. The days lengthen, a screen door slams, and the reassuring message of promise for another colorful summer is heard in Horton Bay.

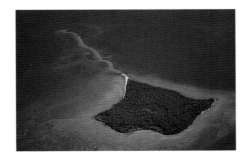

Beaver Island
AMERICA'S EMERALD ISLE

BEAVER ISLAND'S CHARM has captured hearts for many generations and attracts several thousand summer residents and tourists each year. When asked what it is about their Island that they would not trade for the world, the reply comes easily to nearly 400 year-around residents. Serenity, solitude, trust, friendliness, the refreshing smell of pine and cedar, and incomparable sunsets on Donegal Bay are all part of the Island's spellbinding magnetism.

Situated 32 miles northwest of Charlevoix, Beaver is one of twelve islands in the "Beaver Archipelago."

Formed by a glacier that covered North America 11,000 years ago, Beaver Island is thirteen miles long and six miles wide with seven inland lakes. Beaver Island is the largest island in Lake Michigan. It is also the third largest and the most remote inhabited island in the five Great Lakes. Situated 32 miles northwest of Charlevoix, Beaver is one of twelve islands in the "Beaver Archipelago," which includes High, Trout, Squaw, Garden, Hog, Gull, Whiskey, Hat, Pismire, Tim's, and Little Garden Islands, however, only Beaver is now permanently populated.

Native Americans were the first Beaver Island inhabitants, occupying Beaver Island off and on for thousands of years. Although the French voyagers stopped at Beaver Island, it remained unsettled until the 1830s when Europeans arrived from Ireland's Aranmore, County Donegal. The Irish immigrants were nicely settling into a satisfying life of fishing and farming while a renegade community of Mormons was forming in Voree, Wisconsin under the omnipotent leadership of James Jesse Strang. Strang left a very colorful mark on the otherwise quiescent Beaver Island, for it is here that the self-proclaimed king briefly reigned over the only kingdom in the history of the United States.

Strang was born in 1813 on a small farm in New York. When Strang was ten years old, Joseph Smith became founder of the Church of Jesus Christ of Latter-day Saints. Although Strang had no known connections to the Mormon church as a child, in an early diary he expressed grand desires for power and regal position. A lawyer, educated at Fredonia Academy in New York, Strang migrated with his wife and child to Burlington, Wisconsin in 1843. The following year Strang attended a Mormon meeting to hear a galvanizing speech delivered by one of Smith's apostles. It can be debated whether Strang was more intrigued with the Mormon religion or the apostle's ability to captivate his audience in a spiritual

ecstasy. Nevertheless, Strang quickly became a believer, or more precisely saw his opportunity for a future of quixotic glory. He then traveled 200 miles south to Nauvoo, Illinois to be baptized a Mormon.

When Mormon leader Joseph Smith was assassinated in 1844, a four-year power struggle to succeed Smith as leader of the Mormon church ensued between Strang and one of Smith's apostles, Brigham Young. Young and his followers eventually fled Nauvoo to Salt Lake City, Utah while Strang gathered his following at the first Mormon church established by Smith in Kirtland, Ohio. Strang accumulated hundreds of followers, including Smith's mother, brother, and three apostles, persuading them with an elaborate "Divine Revelation" story about being God's chosen successor to Smith.

Strang returned to Voree, Wisconsin and his acolytes joined him there. However, being a man educated in law, with charlatan habits and dictatorial whims, Strang decided it best to move his Mormon community to a more secluded place where he could rule with undisputed sway and be isolated from the laws of the land. Claiming an angel had guided him there, the Mormon Prophet and about twenty-five Mormons arrived by steamer to Beaver Island in 1848.

Hundreds of Mormons soon followed.

A bustling colony ensconced the north end of Beaver Island where the village of St. James still bears signs of Strang's influence. At the peak of Strang's power, approximately 2,600 Mormons occupied Beaver Island. During Strang's reign, which lasted for over eight years, he published the first daily newspaper north of Grand Rapids, Michigan called the "Northern Islander." His political savvy and eloquent manner won him two terms in the Michigan State Legislature where he was admired for brilliant speeches at the State Capital. King Strang proved to be a lascivious man as well. Despite having publicly denounced polygamy, Strang indubitably enjoyed five wives who bore him several children. The King's haughtiness did not bode well with the Irish settlers who soon decamped for the mainland, abandoning the homes and farms they had worked so hard to build.

Under Strang's merciless rule, the Mormons grew increasingly disenchanted in Strang's paradise where the king wandered about in a crimson robe and jeweled crown. The dramatic kingdom of James Jesse Strang came to an end on June 16, 1856 when Strang was ambushed and fatally shot by two of his followers. With news of Strang's death, the jubilant

Irish rushed back to claim Beaver Island – the beautiful place that reminded them of the dense, green forest lands of the Old Country. Without leadership, the remaining Mormons quietly departed Beaver Island for various parts of the country. Today about 100 "Strangites" are based in Independence, Missouri although they are not recognized by the Mormon church.

The prevalent greeting on Beaver Island is "Ceade Mile Failte," Gaelic for "A Hundred Thousand Welcomes."

The only remaining kingdom on Beaver Island is nature's small kingdoms of animal life, although fragments of Beaver's brief sovereign history are still present. The Mormon Print Shop is a Registered Michigan Historic Site that is now operated by the Beaver Island Historical Society as a public museum. Beaver Island's main road is still called King's Highway; its highest sand dune retains the name Mount Pisgah; Jordan is the chief river; the largest inland lake is Lake Geneserath, and the shallow lake at the northern end of the island where King Strang baptized his people is called Font Lake. Indeed, King Strang left his imprint on Beaver

Island and several books have elaborated on the details of this brief and bizarre escapade in American history. However, a more prominent lineage on Beaver Island is found in its Irish history.

The prevalent greeting on Beaver Island is "Ceade Mile Failte," Gaelic for "A Hundred Thousand Welcomes," and this only touches the surface of the Irish roots and friendliness that run deep on Beaver Island. It is believed that Irish immigrants began arriving at Beaver Island between 1832 and 1837. Establishing two major settlements – one at the north end harbor and one at the south end of the Island, known as Cable's Bay – the Irish immigrants earned their living fishing, lumbering, farming, shipbuilding, and working on lake vessels. The island's Marine Museum, an authentic net shed build in 1906, illuminates a time when the St. James harbor swarmed with commercial activity. Beaver Island's population swelled to nearly 2,000, reaching a post-Mormon high, during the peak of the fishing industry from the 1880s to the 1930s. Northern Lake Michigan was a fertile fishing ground until 1936 when the waters became infiltrated with the lamprey eel. This predatory fish decimated native Lake Trout and Whitefish populations. By the time restocking efforts took

hold in the mid-1960s, the island's commercial fishing industry had collapsed and Beaver Island's population fell to an all
time low of 200.

During Beaver Island's boom population period, one of
its most eminent citizens occupied the island. A descendant
of salient educators in Estonia, Feodor Protar came to
America in 1874.
Respectfully referred to
by islanders as "our
Heaven-Sent Friend,"
Protar was educated in
Civil Engineering and
had a career in theater and as a newspaper editor. Although he
traveled extensively before settling alone on Beaver Island in
1893, Protar's real desire was for a new beginning in a quiet
place where he could help others.

Protar never posed as a physician, but he successfully
attended to the simpler health needs of his neighbors and
their animals with his home remedies, always provided free of
charge. A moral, thinking, and articulate man with a long
snow-white beard and hair, Protar lived a minimalist and vir-
tuous life on Beaver Island. Despite appearing to be remote,

*When asking for island
directions a common response is "What
point are you familiar with?"*

he was a very kindhearted soul who generously gave his time
and intelligent advice to those in need.

Protar died just before his eighty-seventh birthday in
1925. Since state law did not allow for Protar's wishes that his
body be slipped into Lake Michigan without any kind of cer-
emony, islanders buried him on his property near his home.
Protar's home and tomb remain as memorials to the man who
was greatly loved and admired by islanders.

Antje Price, a summer islander from Pennsylvania, is
well-known on the island as "The Protar Lady." Price has
exhaustively researched and documented Protar's enigmatic
pre-island life and exalting island life in a series of Journals
published by the Beaver Island Historical Society.

Today, Beaver Island is a much quieter place dotted
with many Irish names that surface frequently in island con-
versation as references to places on the island. When asking
for island directions a common response is "What point are
you familiar with?" Familiarity with island points is akin to
knowing mainland highways and intersections. Kilty's Point,
Sweeney's Swamp, Miller's Marsh, the Stone House, Vesty's
Field, Cross's Landing, Bauman's Bluff, and Mamie Salty's
Clearing are a sampling of the dozens of points and places on

the 53-square mile island, each spot with a history of its own.

Beaver Island's 100 miles of scenic roads, canopied by towering emerald trees, absorbs one in the stark and magnificent beauty of the island. The main highway is paved, but dirt roads skirt over fifty miles of sandy white shoreline and crisscross the interior of the island. The names of cottages, tucked at the end of long, winding driveways – Snug Harbor, Blue Heron, Singing Sands, Serenity – speak to the feelings, sights, and sounds experienced on Beaver Island.

> *The main highway is paved, but dirt roads skirt over fifty miles of sandy white shoreline.*

Wildflowers add splashes of color to Beaver Island and wildlife is abundant. Sightings of deer, owls, rabbit, fox, coyote, loons, herons, beaver, ducks, turtles, American Bald Eagles, and turkeys are common. Because the island has a perfect setting for studying undisturbed habitats, Central Michigan University acquired forty-five acres of land on Sand Bay in 1936. Since 1966, the University has operated a busy Biological Station on the island. Research studies contributing to many Master's Degree theses have been conducted in the

swamps, sand dunes, lakes, forests, rivers, and fields on Beaver Island.

In 1926, deer were planted on Beaver Island from the Belle Isle Zoo. Each fall the Annual Hunter's dinner welcomes those who are about to settle into their island hunting camps and serves as a kick off for the season. Sponsored by the Wildlife Club, the all-you-can-eat wild game feast, donated by islanders, fosters goodwill between hunters and islanders. The Wildlife Club also provides hunting season reports and maintains a wildlife feeding program.

Traditional kindness takes a little time and Beaver Island folks make time for it. Kindness and courtesy are island rules of the roads. Simply flashing vehicle headlights, or gesturing a prolonged wave, to the first person who comes along assures assistance. Of course, patience may be needed, especially during winter months when "rush hour" is defined as seeing more than three cars on the road. The amicable islanders faithfully respect other customs such as never sounding a horn, and passing a vehicle moving in the same direction is a rudeness reserved for the mainland. One of the most pleasant courtesies is the refined "Beaver Island wave." When one approaches another person on

the road, a wave is always exchanged.

Bicycling the island roads, hiking on quiet trails carpeted with pine needles, or strolling through the village is a throwback to earlier days. Clapboard buildings with high false fronts, log houses, weathered barns, aged apple orchards, and posted business hour signs followed by the words "mostly" or "weather permitting" are all part of the island's rustic charm. Although Beaver Island's character is one of north woods natural beauty, its people are not the backwoods kind. The island has its share of interesting, educated, worldly, creative, and resilient individuals who have chosen a quieter way of life and who share a passion for their island. Those who leave the island are often drawn back to its irresistible charm.

The island's annual Homecoming is a popular reunion of past, present, and summer residents, as well as mainland neighbors and tourists. The Homecoming is a festive weekend in August which includes an invitational softball tournament and church dinner and dance. Other island events include the Independence Day parade and fireworks and, of course, Saint Patrick's Day is a celebration of the island's heritage. Museum Week, sponsored by the Historical Society each July, is an activity-packed week of informative lectures,

music, nature walks, and other activities centered around the island's fascinating past.

The island is not without culture and arts. There are Opera Nights, talent shows, and plays performed by a talented cast of island characters. The arts are so appreciated on Beaver Island that the old Dockside Market is being renovated into a state-of-the-art "Beaver Island Community House." Scheduled to open in the new millennium, it promises to be an island centerpiece for the arts and social events.

Another favorite island gathering spot is the Library. Tucked in a natural wooded setting, it is well-stocked with the latest books, periodicals, and technology. With an interior of native cedar and big windows with gorgeous views, it's a comfortable place to hole up for awhile.

In the village, all within an easy walk, are three churches, a Medical Center, bank, museums, stores, restaurants, Fire Department, marinas, post office, softball park, tennis courts, Sheriff's Department, and a park. The Beaver Island Community School, also in the village, is attended by about 100 children in kindergarten through twelfth grades.

Since the island's only bridge to Charlevoix is a boat or a plane, getting to the mainland from Beaver Island requires

time, money, advanced planning, and cooperative weather. The island has two airports with several twenty-minute flights departing and arriving throughout the day. For convenience, many islanders keep a vehicle on the island as well on the mainland.

Always a thrill for islanders, the arrival of the first spring ferry generates a bustle in the harbor as long-awaited freight is unloaded from the boat. The Beaver Island Boat Company operates two passenger, vehicle, and freight ferries out of Charlevoix from April until the end of December. The 95-foot *Beaver Islander,* built in 1962, carries 200 passengers and ten vehicles. The old, tuckered *South Shore* ferry was retired in late 1997 with the arrival of the new *Emerald Isle.* The 130-foot stern-loading Emerald Isle is named for a ferry from years ago. However, the new boat is the grandest ferry Beaver Island has known. She has a capacity for 300 passengers, twenty vehicles and one heavy truck, and is equipped with the latest comforts and conveniences. The Ferry service transports many tourists to

> *Beaver Island is a simpler, less material world. Yet, it is a progressive place.*

and from Beaver Island. The nearly three-hour cruise across Lake Michigan is a wonderful way to make the transition to the slower motion of the island.

Beaver Island is a simpler, less material world. Yet, it is a progressive place. It merely progresses at its own pace, by its own standards, and without sacrificing traditional values along the way. Part of the island's charm is that its residents are more inclined to act on what feels right rather than what might be considered "politically correct" by the rest of the world. Interestingly, much of the rest of the world is racing about, at breakneck speed, desperately seeking some semblance of balance, harmony, and simplicity which are the same qualities that islanders found generations ago. It's an unruffled repose that still exists today on Beaver Island.

Yes, island life has a special quality. It is tranquil, nostalgic, and healing. As day fades into night, there's an ease to the island's silence and a gentleness in its darkness. The moon-washed trees seem to whisper messages from far away. You feel the need to answer, and you cannot, except in spirit. So you drift off to sleep with only the soothing rhythm of the island flowing through you.

Thank You

....

This book could not have been created without the generous assistance of so many people who kindly and enthusiastically shared their knowledge, memories, time, support, encouragement, and places and objects of affection. Our list is long, but you know who you are, and we are grateful.

We extend special gratitude to our fabulous behind-the-scenes team:

Kit Foster

Ted Cline of Photair, Inc.

Corporate Color, especially Joe Hauser

Laura Foster, Editor

Nielsen Design Group - Tim Nielsen, Emily Mitchell and Darren Shroeger

Hal Foster and Trevor & Jane Scott for their understanding, patience, and unconditional love during what must have seemed, at times, a never-ending project.

Finally, we thank each other for our partnership on this journey. Our venture started with a cup of coffee, a sketchy concept, a firm handshake, and a strong desire to merge our creative ambitions. A shared vision emerged during thirteen months of extraordinary collaboration and tireless energy. As we conclude this part of our journey, we take with us many wonderful memories, a treasured friendship, and a photographic essay of an incredibly beautiful region we are very fond of. We leave a book that we hope brings as much pleasure to others as its creation has brought to us.

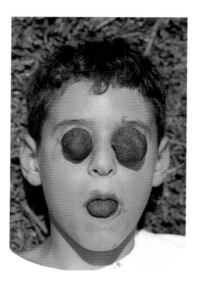